ABOUT THE AUTHOR

Dr. Jane Williams is a clinical psychologist who has worked for over 25 years with individuals who have experienced trauma, life threatening illness, and grief. She completed postdoctoral fellowships at UCLA and Harvard Medical School. At Harvard, she trained in medical crisis counseling and later developed the Medical Crisis and Loss Clinic at Arkansas Children's Hospital. Dr. Williams has helped develop grief programs, made national presentations at grief conferences, and published peer-reviewed articles on grief. She recently retired from Wake Forest Medical School.

CPSIA information can be obtained
at www.ICGtesting.com
Printed in the USA
BVOW06s2058131017
497635BV00011B/55/P

9 781618 460295

Mysterious Moments

Thoughts That Transform Grief

by

Jane Williams, Ph.D.

library partners press
a digital publishing imprint

First Edition, Second Printing

ISBN: 978-1-61846-029-5

Copyright © 2017 by Jane Williams

Cover designed by Library Partners Press

Produced and Distributed By:

Library Partners Press
ZSR Library
Wake Forest University
1834 Wake Forest Road
Winston-Salem, North Carolina 27106

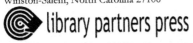 library partners press

a digital publishing imprint

www.librarypartnerspress.org

Manufactured in the United States of America

ABOUT THE BOOK

This book is a collection of 10 stories based on real life experiences of loss. The stories are diverse and involve issues such as the insatiable need for affirmation by our parents, generational family dysfunction, death of an African American male by authorities, compassion burnout, and the effects of cultural attitudes on grieving. Although each story is unique, a common theme ties the narratives together. All of the grievers, despite their distress and suffering, experience moments in which they have transformative thoughts that allow them to reframe their grief. Each person finds meaning through this unconscious process, providing both healing and newfound hope.

ACKNOWLEDGEMENTS

My deepest sense of gratitude goes to the courageous individuals who shared their stories with me. Their openness, often revealing painful memories along with moments of healing, speaks to the resilience of the human spirit.

I am also grateful to all the clients who have allowed me to travel with them on the difficult journey of loss and grief.

The book was originally intended to be a resource for counselors working in the field of grief. However, the late author and biographer, Penny Niven, read one narrative and suggested writing for a much broader audience. She felt the stories had universal appeal and her helpful advice resulted in a book applicable to a wide range of readers.

Special appreciation goes to my editor, Candide Jones, whose corrections and additions gave the narratives more flow and coherence. Additional thanks go to Carol Henderson and Anne Rye for editing assistance and guidance.

Last, but certainly not least, deep appreciation goes to my husband, Roger Kalthoff, who listened patiently, provided valuable insights, and offered encouragement always.

~Jane Williams, Spring 2017

INTRODUCTION

Over the past 25 years, I have been a hospital clinical psychologist, working with children and families experiencing trauma, life-threatening illness, and loss. When I started my career, the literature about grief was in its infancy. Research on grief has increased, but it is difficult work requiring a lengthy investment of time to understand its essence.

Over the years, I have developed a set of beliefs about how people experience grief. Some of these beliefs are supported by research, some are based on theory, and some rely on my clinical experiences. In this set of beliefs, there is one remarkable observation—sometimes people have transformative thoughts that dramatically change their experience of grief. These experiences form the basis for this book.

I believe that grief is a process. In the late 1960s, Elizabeth Kubler-Ross published her first book, *On Death and Dying*,[1] based on research with dying individuals.

Her writings opened the door to a previously undiscussed topic and set the stage for increased understanding of the emotional experience of dying. She outlined psychological stages, including denial, anger, bargaining, despair, and acceptance, which dying individuals may undergo.

Later, these same stages were applied to grieving individuals, with the notion that passage through the phases would result in "acceptance" of loss. The application of the stages of dying to the stages of grieving often led people to expect a prescribed cycle of grief. Grieving individuals understandably felt surprised and disappointed when they did not experience certain set stages. They felt that they had "failed" grief when acceptance didn't arrive on schedule. In my reading, research, and work with grieving individuals, I came to see grief as a dynamic, ongoing process, not an event with a set series of psychological tasks completed in a specific order. Like a meandering stream, the process of grief has a direction and timing of its own.

There are no set time limits for grief. Contrary to many of our cultural expectations, so-called "closure" does not come with the funeral. We cannot "will" grief to start or stop. We want grief to hurry up and end, and we are sometimes perplexed and distressed by its tenacity. Time seems to stand still. As C. S. Lewis wrote, "I not only live each endless day in grief, but live each day thinking about living each day in grief."[2] Early in the process, time feels like an enemy, but as in many processes, time can eventually help us heal and grow.

There *are* common feelings and emotions that may be experienced during grief, but I believe that grief is a highly individualistic process. There is no prediction of how a particular person will respond to a particular loss. In fact, we are sometimes surprised at the strength of emotion that we may feel with a specific loss, yet we are equally surprised with an absence of strong emotion with other losses. Individuals experience loss in their life in unique ways. Some experience intense sadness initially, while sadness comes later for others. For some, sorrow may come in spurts or not at all. Some cry freely and express their distress openly. Others cry in private, hold back tears, or don't even feel moved to cry. Some need to talk constantly about their grief while others are uncomfortable talking about it. Some prefer not to talk but feel better doing tasks or returning to work. Some children cannot concentrate on school tasks, while others throw themselves into their schoolwork. The experience and expression of grief is deeply personal and highly idiosyncratic.

Because of the personal and varying nature of grief, I believe that narratives—stories—are critically important and helpful both for accepting death and coping with loss. Initially, we often need to tell our story of a death over and over to ourselves internally or to others. This helps us assimilate what has happened. It is almost as if we need to imprint the experience to make it real.

I once had a wise mentor who was supervising my work with a patient who kept telling his history over and over. I asked her when she thought he would stop repeating the story. "When he no longer needs to," she said. We are all like this patient: we tell our stories of loss until we no longer "need to."

With the passage of time, the initial narrative often changes, and details are added or taken away. Often the memory of other personal characteristics and relational experiences allow for a more holistic view of the person who died, including both positive and negative qualities. This incorporation of added memories allows us to experience a broader range of emotions involved in the loss. When my father died, my narrative focused on the alleviation of his suffering. He had a very difficult final six months, and I both felt and described his death as a "blessing." With time, my story began to include more memories of our earlier relationship that opened me up to my sadness of his death. My story—*our* stories—change over time and help us accommodate our loss.

Our stories help to make meaning out of loss. In the psychological theory known as constructivism, "meaning reconstruction" is posited as the central process in grief.[3] By creating and telling our narratives, we try to make meaning out of our suffering. The creation of our stories is an active, unconscious process and influenced by both old and new life experiences, such as the birth of a baby in a family following the death of an older child. Over time, our narratives often evolve into a deeper interpretation of our loss experiences.[4] This meaning-making process can result in positive growth for each of us.

Given my belief that grief is an idiosyncratic, meaning-making process with no time limits and best reflected in narratives, I haven't been surprised when grief-stricken individuals tell me of sudden moments when they have experienced transformative thoughts. These "mysterious moments" don't result from a conscious intent; their source is unclear. During these moments, the griever experiences thoughts that reframe his or her grief. They are like the "aha!" moments when, suddenly, we somehow see the world differently. The unexplainable thoughts tend to come "out of no-where," whether the griever is focused on loss or not. The thoughts may occur when our loved one is dying, in the early period following the death, or after many years have passed. They are unique to each individual, weaving together the past and present within the psyche. I find that their occurrence is not universal; they are more often associated with deaths that have caused the bereaved ongoing distress. These thoughts are often breakthroughs that offer relief and healing. This book is written about these meaningful moments, these epiphanies, when individuals suddenly see or understand their loss in a new way.

Here is an example of a transformative moment embedded within a narrative. A father tells of his enduring distress after the death of his adolescent son. His son, who was the team quarterback, died in a car accident after a football game. The son had been his father's delight: he was witty, academically talented, and popular with peers. Two years after the death, the father remained angry and distraught. He had returned to work but continued to have problems concentrating. He had been actively involved in the life of his church, but he gave up his religious commitment and blamed God for his son's death. He was no longer able to hunt and enjoy the out-of-doors that he had shared with his son. Nothing in life gave him any particular joy.

He had a younger daughter with whom he had not shared a close relationship. In contrast to her brother, she was not at the top of her class in academics; she was artistic and not athletic; her boyfriends were not to his liking; and she tended to push the envelope behaviorally. Further, she hadn't been overly demonstrative about her brother's death, and the father interpreted her behavior as not caring about her brother. Their relationship remained rocky until one day when he found a note she had written about her continuing distress over her brother's death and her thoughts of suicide.

The father was shaken. He took immediate steps to seek therapy for them both; he began taking her to lunch and engaging in activities with her; he listened to music she liked; and he talked with her about her boyfriends—even ones he didn't like. One day, while they were walking in the woods where he had previously hunted with his son, he suddenly realized that he had gained a daughter he had never known. In that moment, he understood that he could have lost *both* of his children. Although he continued to mourn his son, he felt a newfound gratitude for his daughter, which helped lessen his distress.

In the pages that follow, you will find narratives of individuals who have experienced loss as well as transformative thoughts that changed the course of their grief. The stories are real, but names and identifying details have been altered. Some of the individuals experienced "mysterious moments" at the time of the death, while others had them years later.

The book is written for a broad audience of readers. For those not presently experiencing grief, the narratives offer an opportunity to better understand a universal process that touches all of us and increases our capacity for compassion.

For individuals in grief, the narratives may decrease the devastating feeling of isolation often experienced during the grieving process. When I worked therapeutically with individual children, I often read a chapter from the book *How It Feels When A Parent Dies* by Jill Krementz.[5] This is a collection of stories in which children of varying ages describe their experiences following the death of a parent. I tried to pick narratives that would closely fit the experience of the child I was seeing in therapy. One day a child looked up at me with tears in her eyes and said, "That girl experienced the same thing as I did. I didn't know there were any other children who felt like I do."

Reading about the experiences of others can decrease this sense of isolation, encourage the sense of survival, and provide a spark to lighten another's path through the dark process of grief.

For counselors involved in grief work, the narratives may be useful. They present opportunities for individuals to talk openly about their own stories of grief.

For all groups, the book was written to offer hope.

CONTENTS

AS
A
MOTHER

AS A MOTHER

Mary Alice opened her worn, red leather billfold and withdrew the old photograph of a thin, sick toddler in denim overalls. There were other "happy" pictures of Hunter in albums and picture frames, but this one showed his suffering. Her son had died before his second birthday, and yet, she had never shared her grief or this photograph of her sick child with anyone else, until now.

Mary Alice Hunter was raised in the Mississippi Delta shortly after the turn of the century, when hard work was prized, and stoicism was a virtue. Children died more often in those days, and there was too much work to be done to sit wallowing in grief. Many women lost several babies, and the implied rule was simply not to talk about it.

The age difference between Mary Alice and her closest surviving sibling was 18 years, and most of her siblings had left home by the time of her birth. She learned self-sufficiency early on.

Her family was "financially well off" in rural Mississippi; her father owned both a dairy farm and a general mercantile store. They were the first and, for a while, the only family to own an automobile. Relative prosperity, however, didn't shield the family from life's hardships, and it wasn't only young children who died. When Mary Alice was two years old, her mother died of uremic poisoning. Like many children who lose a parent early in life, her only memories of her mother were based on stories told by family members. But life must go on: her father, struggling to manage the farm, store, and a two-year-old, soon married her mother's best friend.

There were happy times, however, and Mary Alice remembered her early years as "idyllic" as she spent time chasing animals on the farm and catching crawdads in a nearby creek. Her closest friend was a young African American girl, the daughter of the family's maid. Despite the difference in race—surprisingly at that time in the South—the girls were close, shared many interests, and especially loved playing "church," singing spirituals and passing collection plates.

But heartbreak always seemed to hover close by: a fire destroyed their home, and Mary Alice's family was forced to relocate to town. This was a difficult move for her, as she lost her best friend as well as the freedom she felt living on the farm.

Things settled for a while, but then tragedy struck again: Mary Alice's father died when she turned 13. She didn't know then—and never knew—the cause of his death, but she remembers hearing others say that he "lost his mind." She didn't understand the meaning of this, and, typical of the times, she and her siblings never discussed the circumstances surrounding his death. It was only later that she learned that he had been institutionalized for mental illness.

With his death, the family lost both the farm and store.

After her father died, Mary Alice and her stepmother were alone and facing financial ruin. Her stepmother had never worked outside the home, and, other than farming, the Delta offered few job opportunities. They moved in with Mary Alice's older sister, Elizabeth, herself a widow raising three young boys of her own. Elizabeth relied on her teaching position to provide for her family. It was yet another hard time: her sister's earnings were meager, her stepmother had difficulty adjusting, and Mary Alice was left to raise herself emotionally.

Mary Alice became adept at finding pockets of comfort and stability. As a teenager, she had two primary influences: her family history and playing the piano.

Although she recognized that her reconstituted family was poor, Mary Alice held on to a belief in the importance of lineage. She said, "Although we may not have had money, we had ancestors." Being from a distinguished family who were members of the Daughters of the American Revolution and the Daughters of the Confederacy gave her a sense of importance and place. This notion of "specialness" remained with her the rest of her life.

Her musical talent earned her special opportunities; she played in music festivals and contests, and she won awards for her outstanding ability. Following high school, she received a music scholarship and supplemented her modest financial support by teaching and by taking odd jobs in the college music department.

After college graduation, she was offered an opportunity for further training at a music conservatory in Cincinnati. This precious prospect of a new beginning and expanded horizons wasn't realized, however. She was unable to take advantage of this chance because of the bare bones reality—lack of train fare.

True to her background, she did her best to thrive where she was. She remained in Mississippi, teaching music in the local community and serving as the church pianist for over 50 years. Music was both practical and soothing; it brought her financial benefits as well as comfort and joy.

In 1935, Mary Alice married Walter Smith, a friend since junior high. Walter, a patient man who was wedded to the land, had waited until Mary Alice completed her degree and he had established his own farm. She was 25 and Walter was 27, ages considered "old" for marriage at the time. They lived in the country in a house designed and built by Walter. Her mother-in-law lived next door and was a dominant and domineering force in the family. Mary Alice remembered her as a "harsh literalist" who was guided by punitive scriptures, with little patience for self-pity, and certainly no nurturing "mother figure." As a young married couple, Mary Alice and Walter had limited time together and limited ability to make independent decisions, but they did their best.

Both Mary Alice and Walter loved children and wanted them desperately. Walter was a natural with children, having a gift for entertaining them and making them laugh.

Despite their mutual desire for a family, life again threw obstacles in the way. Mary Alice had four miscarriages and a stillbirth before the joyous birth of their first child, Rebecca, who arrived ten years after their marriage. Mary Alice recalled, "The doctor who delivered Rebecca was almost as excited as we were because it was a live child."

Shortly after Rebecca's birth, Mary Alice was notified of the death of her nephew, William. Of her sister Elizabeth's three sons, all of whom joined the armed forces during World War II, William was her favorite. Shortly before the war was over, William and his unit were caught in the middle of fighting around Remagen, Germany, where a bridge critical for passage of the Allied forces stood. The battle to keep the bridgehead from being destroyed was intense. William had thrown a grenade that killed a number of German soldiers who were trying to blow up the bridge. A grenade was thrown back at William's unit and as it landed, he jumped on the grenade, covering it with his body, and saving his small group of infantrymen. Posthumously, he received the Silver Star for valor. This death affected Mary Alice deeply, and she was struck by the thought that his young life was cut short, robbing him of the future he should have had.

"William never had a chance to live," she said. "He would have made something of himself. He was the cream of the crop."

Despite this sorrow, life again went on, and when Rebecca was eighteen months old, a second child, Hunter Lloyd Smith, joined the family. Finally, Mary Alice thought, the normal joys of ordinary life could be hers.

But within a day of his birth, Hunter was diagnosed with a condition then known only as "blue baby." A "blue baby" lacked oxygen in the blood due to a congenital heart defect, and her precious baby did indeed look blue: his lips, tiny fingers, and toes all had a bluish tint. They took him to Memphis, but no medical interventions were available at the time. Almost nine years later, the condition became known as "Tetralogy of Fallot" and could be successfully corrected by surgery, but at the time of Hunter's birth, it was a fatal diagnosis.

For the next 18 months, the family lived with a dying child. Outwardly, Mary Alice tried to remain upbeat and positive, as she'd learned, repeatedly, from dictated southern social norms. Inside, however, the uncertainty of loss created a landscape of fear, like a time bomb with no set limits, never knowing when it would explode. When Hunter had a good day, she was hopeful, but bad days, and there were many, brought on repressed feelings of despair. She tried to stay busy with chores to block out this emotional roller coaster. She nursed, rocked, and held her child: a child she knew would be hers for an undetermined length of time. She dared not dream about his future.

Her emotions were raw but were invisible to others when they asked about Hunter's condition. She was outwardly calm and polite, but inwardly in turmoil, caught between anger over Hunter's condition and guilt over being angry.

At home, Mary Alice uttered hundreds of unanswered prayers, while Walter walked the floor with their son and tried to make him comfortable. Despite their best efforts, Hunter's suffering became visibly more apparent. His breathing became uneven and unpredictable, and his parents fixedly stared at each rise and fall of his tiny chest. They watched, heartbroken, as his color turned ashen, and he gasped for breath. When death came, it was initially a relief—his suffering was over.

The death of a child is a complicated event, much more so than later deaths which seem at least to be in the natural order of things. Mary Alice and Walter publicly dealt with Hunter's passing by cultivating happy memories of him and always talking about him as constantly cheerful and smiling. They shared pictures of him, playing with toy tractors, and hung a portrait of Hunter with sparkling blue eyes and rosy cheeks in the living room. Their daughter later recalled that Hunter was described in such positive terms that she sometimes wondered if perhaps *she* should have died instead of him.

Although the stress of Hunter's death could have created a rift in their marriage, Walter and Mary Alice actually grew closer together. Wanting more children, they pursued adoption. But Mary Alice always believed that "we never could find anyone who could match Rebecca." She and Walter were so vigilant about Rebecca's safety and so closely monitored her activities that Rebecca became overly cautious herself. In defense of their watchfulness, Mary Alice stressed, "She was the only child we had left."

Mary Alice started teaching at the elementary school, later earning her Master's Degree in early childhood education and eventually becoming the principal of the local elementary school. Outwardly, she appeared successful in both her professional and personal lives. She maintained the façade of the composed, pleasant, southern woman, as her own mother and so many others had. Her way of coping in the world allowed her to manage the daily responsibilities of life, but nothing in her environment took away the distress of her son's loss—not her religion, not her profession, not her family. Her feelings about his death remained raw but unexpressed. She could vividly recall the feel of his tiny fingers on her face and smell his distinctive scent; there was no reconciling his innocence with his suffering.

Her grief never left her, but years after his death, a measure of comfort arrived in an unusual way. One cold evening in 1965, Mary Alice was at home watching the evening news. The brutality of the Viet Nam War was particularly graphic, and the program displayed vivid, disturbing pictures of death and destruction. As she watched, she grieved for all the young men being killed and for their mothers all over the world. She thought of her nephew, William, killed on another faraway battlefield. And she thought of Hunter, who would have been just 18 years of age and newly draft-eligible. Picturing her sweet baby as she often did, suddenly she was struck by the realization that at least he never had to be drafted, or to fight, or to kill, or to *be* killed in a jungle war far from home and family. This notion, after all these years, brought her a peace with his death that she had never experienced before.

Years later, Mary Alice had a visit from one of her daughter Rebecca's friends. They talked at length about Mary Alice's early life and adulthood in Mississippi. Freed momentarily from past cultural norms of stoic silence, Mary Alice removed the picture of her sick child from her wallet and began talking about her son and her grief when he died. She unexpectedly revealed to the young woman the important realization that came as she watched the graphic war footage on television.

"Hunter didn't deserve to die," she said. "But he never had to take another's life. He didn't have to die alone and afraid. His short life was filled with love, and he died surrounded by those who loved him most."

Though Mary Alice's longing for her lost son always remained, that thought had freed her from her suffering. She looked at her visitor and smiled, and she carefully replaced the picture and closed her billfold.

AS
A
GRANDDAUGHTER
AND
NURSE

AS A GRANDDAUGHTER
AND NURSE

Ginger was Paw-Paw's girl, the first of his grandchildren, always his favorite. And the love was mutual: she thought he was beautiful—a larger-than-life man with a booming voice and a deep, full laugh. She loved looking into his surprisingly soft, sad eyes, unusual in such a big, active man.

He loved playing football and had served his country as a captain in the Army. After his stint of building bridges in the military, he sold large earthmovers and farm equipment for a living. Ginger treasured the little green John Deere tractors her grandfather gave her, gifts that fit neatly in her small hands.

One of Ginger's favorite childhood memories was sitting in her Paw-Paw's lap along with his little Chihuahua, "Yogi." She can still feel her grandfather's big hands wrapped around both of them. "Sitting in

Paw-Paw's lap was the safest place in the world," she said. "I loved him more than anyone."

He was more than a man of action. He loved to garden and grew herbs in his yard. An innately curious man, he enjoyed traveling and soaking up information in all types of environments. He read voraciously, liked the ceremony of Catholicism even though he was not Catholic, and highly respected the culture of Native Americans. He was a sensitive man who, at times, battled depression.

When Ginger flashes back to her childhood, she reflects on how her Paw-Paw affected her life. His love had a solidity and dependability that anchored her. Any time she arrived at her grandparents' home for a visit, there was always the joyous greeting of "There's my Ginger!" With each departure, she watched through the back cubby-hole of her parents' Volkswagen Beetle as her Paw-Paw waved from his driveway until they were out of sight.

Despite not always taking care of his own health—both he and her grandmother smoked—he was careful with hers. When she was young, she had asthma. The combination of the smoke, the dog, and a cat with dander exacerbated her breathing difficulties. Paw-Paw made a game out of his protection: when she visited, he often rented a local hotel room and pretended they were on an exciting trip in order to spend time together and protect her health.

He was her mentor, too, teaching her unique skills and an appreciation of nature. When Ginger was working on one of her Girl Scout badges, he taught her how to carve flutes out of bamboo. They hiked in the woods together, where they identified trees by the bark or leaves, picked up mica, and collected arrowheads. Her grandfather had an impressive collection of arrowheads and rocks that he frequently offered her as gifts. She would not take the arrowheads home but rather left them with Paw-Paw for safekeeping. When her only cousin who lived a great distance away came for a visit, Paw-Paw generously offered *him* some of the arrowheads. Ginger was aghast. She thought, "I cannot believe Paw-Paw would give away the arrowheads. Those are mine!" Thereafter, Ginger learned to accept his gifts when offered to her.

Her admiration grew as she did. As a young adult she realized that "he was a salesperson with morals. He would quit jobs over ethical principles; for example, he quit when a dealer wanted to resell a used tractor as new."

During Ginger's teen years, her parents divorced. They had married as teenagers, and Ginger describes them as a "mismatched couple" that tried hard to work out their differences. They had kept their discontent from the children, so the divorce came as a shock and took a serious toll on Ginger. She became quite depressed, dropped out of high school in the eleventh grade, and experimented with drugs. Her behavior started spiraling out of control, and she was headed down a destructive path. She felt hopeless and considered suicide. Yet, she states, "My salvation came in the knowledge that my Paw-Paw loved me more than anyone."

Gradually, and partly because of the stabilizing constancy of Paw-Paw's love, Ginger rebounded, completed her GED, and finished a degree in art. She traveled, took an art workshop in France, and planned to open an art gallery after finishing an advanced degree in art marketing.

While she worked on the advanced degree, however, a confluence of events changed her course. She was financially strapped, and her car had recently been repossessed, though she was waitressing at a restaurant to try and make ends meet. She saw an advertisement on television about a nursing program at the local community college that was within walking distance from her house. The advertisement stressed the virtue of kindness in nursing. Her brother, who had recently joined the Navy, started talking to her about the critical need for nurses in the military.

At the same time, one of her customers at the restaurant asked her what she wanted to do as a career. She told the customer, who happened to be in nursing administration at a local hospital, that she had been thinking about becoming a nurse. The woman invited her to come to the hospital, and Ginger received a royal tour of all the hospital floors and an introduction to the working environment of nursing. She said, "It felt like a calling. I knew I had to be a nurse."

Not long after starting nursing training, Ginger heard that her grandfather had fallen several times and was involved in some fender benders while traveling. She knew it: something was wrong. After a medical work-up, he was diagnosed with a brain tumor, and the recommended intervention was surgery. When Ginger visited him in the intensive care unit, he was hooked up to a plethora of invasive equipment including a nasal-gastric tube and pressure monitor. Ginger, who did not have clinical experience at the time, was horrified. Was this her Paw-Paw? He was awake but not himself. His voice and smell were totally different. Further, because of his nasal-gastric tube, he could not have liquids. He asked Ginger for water, but she reluctantly answered, "No." He looked at her with his soft, sad eyes and said, "I cannot believe that of all the people in the world, you would deny me." Shaken, Ginger left suddenly and did not visit him in the hospital again. Upon his discharge from the hospital, he was taken to a long-term care facility because he was physically too large to be cared for at home.

Ginger never went to see him.

And then she received the call in the middle of the night. Her Paw-Paw had died. She was stunned, both at his death and at the realization that she couldn't remember the last time she'd thought about him. She asked herself, "Why did I not go see him? He would have enjoyed time with me. I was not too busy—I had the time to go." She felt profoundly guilty and could not understand why she did not go. She cried for a couple of minutes but was surprised that she didn't really break down. She expected to fall apart and did not, either then or for many years, understand her absence of emotion.

Ginger didn't make it to the body viewing and straggled in just as her grandfather's funeral was about to begin. The casket was already closed. She insisted that they open the casket so that she could place a jar of dirt and fresh mint, which she brought from his garden, beside him. She wanted things that he loved in the casket with him. Her aunt angrily grabbed her arm and said, "Where have you been? Your grandmother needed you!"

Years later, she could still hear her aunt's angry voice and see images of her grandfather the day after his surgery. Those images of him as he lay there, begging for water, and as he lay lifeless in the coffin, haunted her.

Five years after her Paw-Paw's death, Ginger had completed her nursing degree and was working as a nurse in an adolescent oncology unit. She had become very attached to Nika, one of her teenage patients who had been diagnosed with leukemia. Ginger spent extra time with Nika, nurturing her with her dry wit, making her laugh.

Nika's situation was very complicated: prior to her diagnosis, she had become pregnant, and she decided to keep the pregnancy, despite her illness. She went through chemotherapy, delivered the baby and was raising the child with her mother's help.

Unfortunately, Nika relapsed and had to have further chemotherapy, radiation, and dialysis. Despite all the medical attempts to save her, she was dying. Her mother, who had been extremely supportive of her daughter during initial treatment, was surprisingly absent and really no longer there for her daughter. Nika spent days by herself, crying constantly and calling out for her mother. Her mental capacity became diminished, and eventually she could not care for herself, lying in bed in diapers.

Prior to her decline, Nika's mother had left instructions that she wanted everything done for her daughter, including all attempts to save her if she required immediate resuscitation. Ginger, however, had witnessed many of these "Code Blue" situations in the past and knew how physically invasive and often damaging or useless they were for the patient.

When Nika's heart stopped beating, her mother was not present; there was no signed consent for withdrawal of care, and her chest was cracked open in an attempt to resuscitate her. She aspirated, was cognitively devastated, and required a breathing tube to stay alive. Nika remained in the intensive care unit for days before her death. Ginger describes the death as terrible. She drowned in her own bile.

Ginger went to Nika's funeral, feeling angry about the mother's absence and critical in general of parents with terminally ill children who did not spend more time with their dying children.

When Nika's mother arrived at the service, her grief was palpable. She cried hysterically, called her daughter's name, and required support to remain standing. Her distress was so intense that it appeared that she had to consciously make herself breathe.

Somehow, at that moment, Ginger's anger was transformed by the realization that being present with her dying child had been too painful for Nika's mother. She felt that she was not a good mother if she didn't insist on everything being medically done for her daughter. Watching the heartbreaking, inevitable advance of her daughter's death on a daily basis was too difficult. It was more than she could bear.

In this same moment, Ginger thought about her Paw-Paw. She was struck with the idea that she, too, could not watch the dying of the hero of her childhood. She could not bear to hear the person, who at one time had kept her alive, beg for water. It was too much for her at that unsettled point in her life's journey.

She began to embrace the notion that she had avoided him not because she didn't care, but because she did not know what to do and could not watch him die. At that moment at Nika's funeral, she forgave herself. She realized that sometimes the people who appear most distant might in fact be hurting the most.

After Nika's funeral, Ginger thought about and still missed her grandfather, but the images of him in the intensive care unit and coffin stopped. They were replaced by happier memories of earlier times spent together—of his little gifts, of his care.

When Ginger's grandmother later developed lung cancer, Ginger stayed with her. She took her to chemotherapy and, by that time, knew how to take care of her nursing needs. This time, she knew what to do: they read *People* magazine together, ate pizza and drank beer, spent time in the hot tub, and talked for hours on end.

Ginger was even able to help her own mother become more comfortable with caring for her dying grandmother. Her grandmother died peacefully at home. Ginger's new acceptance of her own limitations at a young age, and finally forgiving herself for them, allowed her to give herself and her own mother the gift of caring for someone they loved.

In a way, it was Paw-Paw's final and most important gift to her.

AS
A
SISTER

AS A SISTER

Jackie was born and raised on the West coast, the daughter of a librarian and a college educator. Her parents were "liberals" who focused on education and diverse cultural experiences for their children. At the dinner table, there were nightly political discussions and according to Jackie, "I was raised on NPR."

The family lived in a multi-ethnic neighborhood, and the children learned to speak Spanish fluently from their nanny. Yet, even with their neighborhood and school diversity, Jackie realized from an early age that Black children, especially Black males, faced special challenges in order to be safe in the world. She often feared for herself and her siblings.

Jackie was the oldest of the three children, and she took on the role of "junior mom" for her younger siblings. Sharon, the middle child, was a free spirit, while Marcus, the youngest sibling, was the athletic star of the family. Jackie was close to her siblings but often related to them more as caretaker than as sister.

Marcus was extremely active and intellectually sharp. Jackie described him as "happy go lucky" until the age of 20. Then things changed. During his sophomore year in college, he made his first suicide attempt and was diagnosed with bipolar disorder. His life spiraled and was typified by difficult relationships, dependency on his parents, repeated hospitalizations, and multiple arrests. During his manic episodes, his vocabulary was peppered with four-letter words; he had paranoid thoughts about family and friends; and often his physical appearance revealed the rough life he was living.

Bipolar disorder is a cyclical illness, and there were peaceful, productive stretches of time when Marcus had no apparent problems. He was successful in several colleges and eventually earned multiple degrees. He was witty and creative—he published his writings in college newspapers, and his irreverent humor often riled up his readers. He loved quoting from old movies and often made his family laugh with pertinent quotes that fit particular situations. Once, when Jackie was having difficulty with a colleague at work, Marcus commented, "We can keep it classy or get down with gangster shit."

Unfortunately, the side effects of his medication, including weight gain, a tremor, blunted humor, and simplistic thinking robbed Marcus of the qualities he thought most defined him. And yet, not taking his medication brought back the confused thought and erratic behavior.

During this time, Jackie finished her undergraduate and master's degrees and worked internationally in public relations. Her career was quite successful, but she saw that often women in high administrative positions didn't have families. She wanted marriage and children, so she decided to make career and life changes.

Jackie creatively changed her career focus, married, and had a son. Throughout these years, her communication with Marcus was intermittent and, at times, extremely distressful. It went from periods of non-communication to times she would mediate with landlords and college officials for him, reprising her caretaker role.

One night, Jackie found Marcus sleeping on the floor with no blankets and no food in his apartment. He was thin and complained that because he couldn't sleep, he was running 10 miles a day, mainly at night. This stirred her old fears of cultural prejudices against young Black males. Marcus was an athletically built young adult, naïve about others' misperceptions, so she made him promise not to run after dark.

Sometimes, Marcus was grateful for her help; other times, he was verbally abusive. In one conversation,

Marcus told Jackie, "Bitch, you think you know everything and are laughing at me behind my back. You are a terrible person, and our parents don't love you." Jackie became mentally fatigued dealing with Marcus and often wondered when the phone rang, "What brother am I going to get?"

Jackie believed that Marcus never accepted his diagnosis and constantly ran from it. Much of their conversation was about positive days before his illness. She felt that he couldn't reconcile the person he had become with the person he had been.

Marcus valued wealth and would plot and scheme for money. "The reality was that there was a big gap between who he was and who he wanted to be," Jackie said. She loved him but was angry with him for his refusal to go to therapy and stay on his medication.

With age, Marcus seemed to be slowly disintegrating. His high and low cycles became more frequent, and he had greater difficulty rebounding. He moved home with their parents, but Jackie said, "He was like a caged lion. He was up all night slamming doors." His behavior was erratic and menacing, and she feared for her parents' safety.

In one of his more stable periods, Marcus enrolled in a graduate program to enhance one of his degrees and moved into campus housing. But then he stopped taking his medications and began hallucinating. One night, he was asked to leave the college library because he was loud and creating a disturbance. He went back to his apartment and called the police to say that he needed help.

When the campus police arrived, he was barefoot and asked to put on his shoes. Without waiting for the crisis team for assistance, the campus police refused his request, and Marcus became combative. The police tried to cuff him, a struggle ensued, and he was shot five times and killed.

When the family received the autopsy report, the pictures revealed bruising all over his body, suggesting recent mistreatment. For unknown reasons, his body wasn't released to the family for two weeks, further intensifying their grief.

The last time Jackie heard from Marcus was a month before his death. He had called asking, "Can you send me some pictures of my nephew? Don't forget." A month later she received the early morning call about her brother's death. He had been shot, but there were no other details. She became hysterical and fainted twice.

A day and a half after Marcus' death, Jackie had her sixth miscarriage. The fertility treatments had been brutal, and she felt punished by God for the loss of her brother and her baby.

Jackie's grief was intense and debilitating. She had to make lists just to get through the day—feed child, do laundry, pick up mail, take a bath, remember to breathe. "It was like being thrown down to the bottom of a well. It was cold and dark. The sides were smooth, and I couldn't crawl up. I didn't know how I was going to get out," she said. She felt profoundly despondent and described her sadness as being so extreme that she experienced physical pain.

The nature of her brother's death intensified her grieving. In contrast to loss that comes from illness or accidents, social support is dampened when the death is violent. No one seems to know what to say, and those in grief feel not only anguish but also intense social isolation.

Jackie's consciousness of the impact of race, present from her early childhood, led her to believe that Marcus would still be alive if he had not been Black. He was doubly vulnerable. First, police are often not prepared to deal with individuals with mental illness. Their strange behavior provokes fear in authority figures. Second, the cultural narrative about young Black males insinuates that Marcus somehow must have been aggressive and violent. He must have done something wrong to cause his death.

One effective survival strategy for Jackie was to write a blog post. E-mails poured in and she found a "community of suffering" that she didn't know existed. She felt embraced by others who had similar experiences and had survived. She realized that she would survive, but she knew she needed more than simple survival—she knew she had to face her grief. She could not push it away and hope it would disappear. She believed there had to be some meaning to her suffering.

Jackie continued to grieve for both Marcus and the multiple children she had lost through miscarriage. She and her husband were determined to have another biological child, and she thought, "If I just work hard enough, I can make it happen." She described her tenacity as both an asset and character flaw resulting in a constant cycle of expectation, attempt, and letdown. Eventually, she tossed the syringes in the trash and donated the rest of her medication to the fertility clinic. She said, "I was tired of seeing my abdomen black and blue from injections. I was mentally wearing down."

Two years after Marcus died, she and her spouse decided to pursue adoption through foster care. The social workers minced no words about how difficult the process would be and told horror stories about some of the children's behavior including lying, swearing, stealing, and excessive masturbating. The program was not for the "faint of heart."

Children coming into foster care presented a multitude of challenges, and often, their parents did as well. Most of the children had parents whose rights had not been terminated, and, many times, foster parents would be co-parenting with biological parents. Adoption, if it came, would be a slow process.

The foster care-to-adoption program included in-depth interviews, classes that explored motivations for fostering and adopting children, and sessions that focused on potential foster parents' histories of losses. Potential foster parents had to discuss their experiences of loss in class, write about them, and talk about them during the home evaluation.

During one of the classes focused on loss, Jackie had a sudden realization that permanently altered her grieving for Marcus. "I can totally handle this challenge," she thought. "Not only do I have the ability, but I am also the perfect person to do it. I can love and take care of a traumatized child. I would never have been able to do this without the resilience I have experienced since the death of my brother. The suffering that I have known over the last two years has prepared me for this journey."

A piece of her soul had died when Marcus died. But the sudden awareness of her newfound strength allowed her to put the pieces back together in a uniquely healing way, making it possible for her to successfully foster a child.

AS
A
SON

AS A SON

John is short and stocky with snow-white hair and facial stubble. He has penetrating blue eyes and a ruddy complexion—the kind of man that conjures up images of Santiago in Hemingway's *Old Man and the Sea*. A lone earring adds to his rugged sensuality. He doesn't look like a pacifist who marched against the Viet Nam and Iraq wars, nor a scholar with a Ph.D. in chemistry who worked as a researcher and teacher before retirement. His looks belie his politically liberal activism and deep longing for peace.

The youngest of eight children, John was born in upstate New York. When he was an infant, the family moved to a farm in Iowa. His father had been a teacher, but times were difficult, and farming was an option. John's father worked incredibly hard to make a living off the land and to provide for his family.

Unfortunately, John's strongest childhood memory was of his father's verbal abuse, both of his mother and of the family in general. His father became enraged over inconsequential words or events, and his frightening voice would rise with his fury. He constantly created uproar, and his rants seemed unending; once he started, he would recount a litany of perceived past wrongs.

None of the children had positive feelings about their father. Unsurprisingly, two of the older boys left home before completing high school. One worked as a farmhand nearby but seldom came home. The other son, though underage, joined the Marines as a means of escape.

John never felt close to his father and was extremely bitter toward him. A major source of John's bitterness was the hypocrisy between his 'church father' and his 'home father.' His father was a devoted member of the local Lutheran Church and incredibly knowledgeable of scripture. He would quote Biblical passages to John anytime he thought his son erred. Considered to be a pillar of the church, his father taught Sunday school and served on the nominating committee when a new pastor was needed. Other than a few skirmishes with more liberal church members, he demonstrated "saintly" behavior at church.

At home, his father was just the opposite—controlling and demeaning. John recalled one Sunday when his father was angry because the children spilled and scattered ashes from the coal stove on the floor. This minor incident set his father off, ranting and raving at John's mother. When they arrived at the church, John said, "Let's act like a real Christian family." John's father became furious, walked away from the family and went inside the church.

His father's reaction upset John, and he started to cry. Inside the church, his tears were ignored, and his father's two faces remained a secret. Feeling isolated, John told a close church friend, "Things are not as they seem in our family."

John's mother held the family together. She was a gentle soul who nurtured all the children, and they adored her. She was compassionate and warm with a wonderfully shy, disarming laugh. She was open and easy to talk with about any subject from sex to circumcision. A sensitive child, John often sat on a stool at the end of the kitchen workbench while she cooked, just so he could be in her presence and ask her questions. His mother listened with such depth that John knew he had been heard. She accepted his fears and made life bearable.

A childhood story involving the Rapture captures John's love of his mother and loathing for his father. The Rapture is a belief held by some Christians that true believers will be elevated to Heaven at the Second Coming of Christ with non-believers left behind. John had been to revival services full of damnation and talk of the Rapture, and he was terrified of the Second Coming. His fears of having a different sexual orientation and guilt over masturbation lead him to believe that there was something dysfunctional about him. He was sure he had committed some unpardonable sin, and, no matter how much he prayed, he would not be redeemed. He was sure, however, that his mother would be taken into heaven because of her goodness.

One morning shortly after the revival, John was in the barn milking cows with his father. His father sent him to the house to get his mother for the cream. John called for his mother, but she didn't respond and couldn't be found. He asked himself, cold with terror, "Where could she be? Has the Rapture happened and taken her?" Then he thought, horrified: "The Rapture has come and taken my mom. Now, I am stuck with Dad."

No one in the family ever defended his father's behavior. John's sisters tried to persuade their mother to leave, but she would never consider it. Earlier in the marriage, she had taken all the children and gone to her family to get away from the situation. But, during the trip, two of the children were diagnosed with whooping cough, developed pneumonia, and died. Her guilt from that experience closed the door to any escape.

As much as she loved her children, she never asserted herself during her husband's tirades and never addressed the difference between his church and home behavior. This pattern was lifelong for her. Even at the time of her death from cancer, she was found crying over her husband's hurtful words.

After her death, John's father left the farm and moved into a retirement community. Though he had remained harsh with his wife until she died, now he made a surprising change in his behavior. He began to mellow and ultimately developed a warm and affectionate relationship with his grandchildren. He invited his older grandchildren to go to dinner with him and engaged them in games, especially chess.

John, who had seen little of his father due to service in the Air Force and college, recalled, "I saw someone that I did not recognize. Somehow, my father had drastically changed." The transition was confusing; without an explanation, his father had softened from being hard and judgmental to being kinder and more thoughtful.

John's first son, David, was born on his father's birthday, and his father drafted a touching letter that is now a treasured keepsake for John. With elegant penmanship, his father wrote about how happy he was with John and his daughter-in-law's life together and about his thrill that David was born on his grandfather's birthday. The letter demonstrated, in words, a whole new side of his father that John had never known.

Shortly after David's birth, John's father had a life-threatening bleed in his femoral artery. His surgery was successful, but he feared being transferred to an extended care facility. Against hospital orders, he got up in the night and fell in the shower.

John and his family received the news of his father's surgery and raced to see him, but he died shortly before they arrived. The suddenness of his father's death was painful and traumatic for John. Despite their contentious relationship, he grieved intensely, and for months, he would break down and cry when alone. His sadness disrupted all aspects of his life.

As he struggled with his grief, John initially wondered if his intense reaction was due to the unresolved animosity between them. As he continued to reflect, the idea struck him that he was like his father in some ways, especially when he reacted with anger at the little things his children did. When he thought about this behavior, he acknowledged, "I am my father." He had never understood the origin of his father's anger, and now he was puzzled by his own behavior.

Although John had known his father's childhood history, the significance of it suddenly became clear. John recognized that his father had carried around a burden of hidden pain that had resulted in striking out at the wrong people. John's father had lost his own father as an infant. The family was destitute, and John's father was, for the most part, abandoned as a young child.

During childhood, John's father had been frequently farmed out as a laborer to nearby neighbors, who often took advantage of him. Worse, his mother didn't protect him from these situations. When she remarried, his stepfather did not accept him, and she did not shield him from his stepfather's disdain. The more he thought about his father's childhood sorrows, the more he realized how painful these early experiences were for his father, and how he carried that pain silently within him.

John also began to believe that he was partly culpable for their relational divide. He described himself as a "self-absorbed teenager" who did not want to be around his father. He only reluctantly helped with necessary chores on the farm and avoided any extra work that might alleviate his father's burdens. Eventually, John realized that "we are all broken to various degrees and we often carry that brokenness around like a rock on our back without acknowledging or sharing it."

Yet, even with these insights, John continued to feel deep ambivalence as he simultaneously grieved deeply and held on to his long-standing bitterness toward his father. He was afraid that the bitterness could destroy him.

But one day, years later, John was working in his garden, and a sudden thought came to him. He surprised himself by speaking to his father, both forgiving him and asking for forgiveness. "Dad, I am sorry for the ways that I failed you when you needed me. I have a lot of pain from our past, but I forgive you. Will you forgive me?"

From that moment on, John began to feel a release from his suffering and anger. He was never sure if his negative feelings resolved or simply went to a place where they no longer hurt. But John could now truthfully say, "I loved my father through all the crap and brokenness."

Somehow, that unexpected moment in the garden had healed the broken relationship. Making peace with his father allowed John to become a pacifist in the truest, deepest sense—a peacemaker both in the world and within his own soul.

AS
A
PHYSICIAN

AS A PHYSICIAN

In Catherine's office, the vibrant back wall is covered with brightly decorated ceramic objects—butterflies, salamanders, crabs, moons, fireflies, and fish. The simple forms and intense colors are reminiscent of Central American artwork. On the opposite wall hangs a framed quote from E. J. Carstensen: "The real meaning of 'physician' is not clear until one must comfort without hope of cure." There is a sense of both the joy and seriousness of life in her surroundings.

A neonatologist practicing neonatal palliative care, Catherine carefully opens a desk drawer and takes out a small box banded by a metallic thread tied in a bow. She eases the thread off and removes the lid. Inside is a diminutive silver disk on a tiny braided chain. It will be given to a mother whose baby dies in the Neonatal Intensive Care Unit (NICU). The child's name will be engraved on the necklace and on a small coin imprinted with tiny footprints that will be given to the father. These are concrete remembrances of their child—a child who will always be their child.

These tiny remembrances are not all; some meaningful mementoes are specially made even before a child's birth. Catherine connects expectant mothers whose unborn children have been diagnosed prenatally with a terminal condition with volunteer seamstresses. Together, they create a special outfit for the child. This idea came from a mother who lamented that she would never buy a prom or wedding dress for her daughter, but only a baptismal/burial dress.

These are two concrete examples of the program that Catherine has developed to build a community of support for parents who experience the death of a child. Along with these remembrances, she also trains physicians in how to support families encountering end of life experiences.

Catherine changed her personal approach to families after her first involvement in a child's death but later realized that changing her personal practice wasn't enough.

"The approach to a family should not be dependent on a specific physician being on service, but all physicians need to be capable of helping the family transition into a meaningful death for their child," she thoughtfully said. "We should not just insert tubes into a baby and then walk away when our procedures don't work. There is a need for change in medicine's approach to a dying child—a need for a standard of care in which medical providers create a sense of community and caring for the family.

"Programs need to be created in which physicians have time to meet with families from the beginning of a diagnosis, engage in honest conversations, work on any disconnect between the physician and family, and provide a sense of support during and after the dying process," she further explained. "There are critical ways of taking care of the family beyond medical interventions."

Catherine grew up in a working class family in Ohio and her mother, an elementary school teacher, was the first woman in her family to go to college. There was no family history of medical careers, and Catherine knew no doctors except her pediatrician. Because she was smart, people told her that 'she should be a doctor.' "Most of what I learned about medicine was on television," she said, laughing.

There was something in Catherine that always wanted to help others, and her family fostered this value as well. They participated in clothing and food drives, and Catherine remembered, "My mother would do anything for anybody."

Catherine attended an all-girls Catholic high school that focused on service projects, and Catherine would take the bus to a dangerous part of town to work in a community house for children. Her mother, who always encouraged Catherine to experience the world, never said a discouraging word to her adventurous daughter. "I always seemed to seek out experiences that gave me a bigger picture of human endeavor," Catherine said.

After high school graduation, Catherine entered St. Louis University, a Jesuit institution that stressed the importance of making the world a better place. She studied both medicine and social work and, during the summers, traveled to Central America on mission trips. In Honduras, she lived in an orphanage. She felt drawn to the care of children and their need for family ties.

Both in the classroom and in the real world, Catherine learned about liberation theology that focused on Christ's relationship with the poor. She was strongly influenced by the work of Dorothy Day, a leader of the Catholic worker movement, who emphasized the importance of making structural changes in systems that keep people in poverty.

Catherine finished college with two degrees, one in biology and the other in theology. She was torn about which path to follow and applied to only one medical school. She decided that if accepted, she would attend; if not, she would earn a Ph.D. in theology.

Accepted to medical school, she found the training different from what she expected as she spent most of her waking hours studying. "I missed human interaction and nearly quit until I took a humanities course on death and dying which involved work with patients at Hospice," Catherine reflected. "This experience, along with meeting my future spouse, turned my medical education around."

Catherine was accepted for both her residency training and a fellowship in pediatric neonatology in San Antonio. "We had a special patient population," she commented. "Many were undocumented immigrants and only spoke Spanish. Since I knew Spanish and had worked in Central America, the interaction with patients was very positive for me."

During her training, she observed attending physicians caring for newborns, but she was never totally responsible for these tiny patients. As she neared the end of her fellowship, she fearfully realized she would soon be solely reliant on her own skills for their care.

Her first "in charge" experience came while working on the transport team of the medical center. She flew by helicopter to a hospital in a city near the border to pick up a newborn with severe hypoxic ischemia encephalopathy, a condition resulting from a lack of adequate oxygen to the brain.

The full-term baby looked beautiful, since the severity of his condition was not yet visible. Once Catherine medically stabilized him, she took him to his mother's room for her to see and hold. Catherine talked with the mother about where her son would be going and reassured her that she would remain with him. The two women immediately bonded—one who had given birth, the other who would care for the child.

The mother had required an emergency Caesarean section and was medically fragile, and she could not be released from the hospital or travel with her son. Her only connection to her newborn was through Catherine. During the next few days, Catherine vigilantly remained beside the infant in his warmer.

Despite all her medical interventions, the baby developed seizures followed by complete respiratory failure, necessitating a breathing tube to sustain his life. He was clearly not improving, and his downward spiral grew to include multiple organ failure.

Catherine sat by his bed and repeatedly called his mother with updates about his condition and care. She had to give his mother the difficult news that if he survived, he would not walk, talk, or eat on his own due to the severity of his condition.

Eventually, his body shut down, and Catherine had to tell his mother that he would not survive. They cried together on the phone, and the mother said that she wanted his suffering stopped. Catherine was able to keep the baby alive until the parents arrived. She worked with the parents to arrange a baptism and compassionate removal of his breathing tube. The death was devastating for the young parents.

Over the next several weeks, Catherine found herself crying at home. She experienced the same helplessness and guilt that she had felt at the baby's bedside. She questioned if there were other things that she could have done. She wondered out loud, "Even with all this training, all these machines, all these medications, and all these procedures, nothing made this baby better." She could not take care of the family in the way that she wanted; she could not heal him with her technical skills. Her grief was raw and ever-present.

And then suddenly, one morning, the thought came to her that maybe just being present had been enough. She had walked the path with the family in a different way. There were limits to what she could do physically for the baby, but perhaps the listening, crying, affirmation, and compassion were enough to help them withstand their loss and pain.

Catherine thought, "When a baby is dying, it is not that there is nothing else that I can do. I can transition my care of the baby so that the family can have a meaningful death in the midst of the most horrible situation a family can ever experience. I can support the family, deliver compassionate care, make available the opportunity for pictures and baptism, and provide bereavement mementos." She no longer felt helpless, but saw she could help in a unique and necessary way.

Several months later, the parents came to a bereavement meeting at the medical center. The medical staff explained in greater depth the baby's condition and answered the parents' lingering questions. Catherine was present and participated in the discussion.

After the meeting, the parents gave Catherine a tiny angel statue encased in glass and a card that expressed their appreciation for her care. Their feedback was focused on her compassion and kindness, not on her medical expertise. Catherine and the mother hugged each other and cried.

The small statue and card have made five moves with Catherine since her medical training and occupy a special place on her bookshelf.

These tokens, as well as the silver disk and tiny coin, are tangible symbols of the spiritual meaning of her work. "I honor children and their families by allowing myself to feel deeply for them and by creating a safe space for both joy and sorrow," she said.

AS
A
FAMILY
MEMBER

AS A FAMILY MEMBER

Margaret works patiently in her side yard on a skin-on-frame kayak that she is constructing out of yellow pine. She has named it "Skipper" in memory of her older brother, Skip. It will take a year to construct, but she has developed patience over time due to the many hardships she has endured.

Margaret, the youngest and only girl in a family of five children, said she had an idyllic childhood. She and her older brothers had everything they materially needed and lived in a wealthy suburb—perfect for kids. There were safe, dead-end streets where children could play games, ride bikes, explore nearby woods, and swim in a neighborhood pool.

The neighbors were educated freethinkers, and their family was no exception. Their mother was creative and funny. She encouraged imaginary play with her children, took them on field trips, designed art projects, and stimulated their curiosity. She taught them to question and think about issues.

Their father, an Ivy League professor and medical researcher, was a distant, difficult man who was largely absent. He financially supported the family but traveled frequently to lecture, attend conferences, and develop research projects. When home, he worked long hours. He was internationally engaged: Margaret remembers his bringing back Southeast Asian children for local physicians to treat, with one staying with them for a short time. But he was disengaged with his own family. He was brilliant and successful, she said, but a "stranger" who came and went.

His emotional distance wasn't the worst of it, though. He was abusive. "He hurled insults toward our mother and referred to me as a 'wench,'" she recalled. "There were very different rules, based on gender, in our family." Her father had little respect for women, had numerous affairs, and even brought a young woman to their house when their mother was away. And it wasn't only the females who suffered: once, her enraged father took one of her brothers to the end of their cul-de-sac, pulled his pants down, and beat him.

No one, however, ever spoke about any of this behavior. Silence was the unspoken rule.

Margaret's older brother Skip was her caretaker. Their mother told Skip, "You do not need to be jealous or resentful of the baby because she is *your* baby." Skip's caring for Margaret formed the basis of their relationship. He did a good job and taught her how to jump off a stone wall and land without hurting her knees, how to sew, and how to put together jigsaw puzzles. They particularly enjoyed construction projects.

Margaret looked up to Skip and, as a small child, felt connected to him. But after puberty, he began to tease her, punch her, and push her around. He could be kind and generous but began to show a callousness that was all too familiar in the family. "It became all about power and gender," she said, "perpetuating patterns that we had seen and known."

Margaret was sent off to boarding school at the age of 12, and the family dispersed as her parents moved to the West Coast, and her siblings attended college or boarding schools.

When she was home on vacation, her father's behavior took an even more frightening turn: her father sexually abused Margaret several times when she was a young teen.

And the family code of silence held fast.

Years later, she attempted to break the silence by writing a letter to her parents describing his behavior, but her father insisted that her story was ridiculous—she had made it up. He described her as "disturbed." The rest of the family accepted his side of the story and asked no further questions. Unsurprisingly, her relationship with her father ended with few words exchanged before his death.

Despite all the turmoil, and despite Skip's cruel treatment, Margaret still had a relationship with him. When she started college, Skip was in graduate school, and living close to each other, they spent some of their summer months together. Their relationship as young adults was "odd" with a lingering, confusing residue left over from childhood. Although they still shared interests and activities, the relationship had jagged edges.

Margaret wanted to expose and reject those pieces, but she had no experience, no idea, how to do it. And the damage continued to spread. Margaret saw that he treated his girlfriend dismissively and rudely. When she tried to talk to him, he became angry and insisted that his behavior was none of her business.

Following graduation, Skip moved to the Middle East and married a woman from Dubai. He and his wife had five stair-stepped children, the oldest of whom was six years old when they moved to the United States.

By this time, Skip and Margaret hadn't spoken for several years. Their relationship was cordial but not connected. When he returned to the states, he lived near Margaret, and she joined him as he looked for property for both family and business purposes. They had a good time looking at real estate, yet Margaret was aware that his wife was trapped in an apartment with five young children. Margaret soon realized that her brother was "mean and demeaning to his wife."

"I felt guilty for enjoying my time with Skip at the expense of my sister-in-law," she said. "But I did not call him on his behavior, as I knew it would be the end of our fun."

Skip was financially successful. As a child, he had wondered how he could make money and have a privileged life style. His goal was to become a millionaire. And he made it happen. As an adult, he acquired considerable property and accumulated significant wealth. Going along with this status, he always felt entitled. For example, he would go to the front of any line without any apologies.

Skip provided well for his children and afforded them enriching experiences and opportunities, just as his father had for him. Unlike his father, though, he spent time with the children and attended to their needs. Nevertheless, Margaret realized that Skip was recreating the same family dynamic of their childhood. The difference between the public versus private persona for both her father and Skip was striking. Outwardly successful and responsible, they were both abusive and controlling in intimate relationships.

One of Skip's children was different and difficult, and he seemed to be missing something important in social relationships. From the age of two years, Michael reacted intensely to the world, and his behavior was odd and often out of control. Skip frequently overreacted to his son's behavior, which created even greater chaos and distress. Margaret remembered, "The other children in the family had to tolerate significant discomfort related to parental conflict in dealing with Michael."

Ever arrogant, Skip thought he could handle Michael's behavior himself. He refused to consult with experts or explore information on parenting. When a teacher tried to pursue a diagnosis and treatment for Michael, Skip took the school district to court. He resisted all efforts at intervention. By the time he was 12, Michael threatened his mother with a knife. At 18, while in a rage, he stabbed Skip eight times. Skip hemorrhaged and died from massive blood loss.

Margaret had spent time with Skip a few months before his death and had an intuition that something "weird" might happen. Things in the family were tense, and Michael's behavior remained threatening. He had made several attempts to harm his father over the summer. Margaret intended to call her brother with some ideas about how to calm the situation, but, ultimately, she said nothing. The family code of silence somehow remained.

Margaret's reaction to Skip's death was complex; it did not fit neatly into a box. She was profoundly sad, mourned him deeply, and couldn't think of him without crying. She was simultaneously angry at her nephew *and* at her brother for not seeking help for his son. Yet, in all her emotional turmoil, she continuously asked herself, "How do I reconcile his loss with holding him accountable?" Skip had been part of a cycle of violence, both as perpetrator and victim. She had lost her relationships with her father, her brother, and her nephew to this insidious cycle. She desperately asked herself, "How do we stop it? How do we keep it from happening?"

Eighteen months after Skip's death, the siblings planned a family gathering at a brother's home in Virginia. Driving to the gathering through the mountains of Appalachia, Margaret found herself meditating about variations in the culture and landscape surrounding her. She contemplated the concept of a broader community that cut across geography and people over time. Somehow, there was connectivity in what seemed to be so disconnected.

Suddenly, she realized that the pain experienced across the generations in her family was rooted in poisonous silence. Having identified silence as the cause of so many broken relationships, she decided the family didn't have to experience further loss. This awareness immediately decreased her distress over the senselessness of her brother's death. She suddenly understood that the only way to stop the cross-generational cycle of mistreatment was open, honest communication. She believed that her relationship with her living siblings could change, even in a family unaccustomed to talking openly and intimately.

Margaret knew that this transformation might or might not happen, and even if it happened, it would be a slow process. But she was determined. The gathering became her first attempt to change the family dynamics. Afterwards she admitted, "I did not obtain the level of openness that I wanted, but what my siblings said was 'real' enough."

In going home, she knew that there would be no turning back. This would be an enormous change for her, as it was totally alien from her family's training in "how to be in relationships."

Margaret was acutely aware that she had played a part in the code of silence by ignoring behavior that she found egregious. She could no longer tolerate the notion that if she could not change something, she did not address it. "If I see something, I have to name it," she said. "I did not achieve anything I wanted by not saying anything."

And the transformation went beyond dealing with her family. By directly communicating with people, she began trying to change the culture at her work, with her friends, as well as with her siblings. She believed that she might make meaning out of the lost relationships with her father, her brother, and her nephew by breaking the silence.

The kayak she is constructing is one other way she is communicating. By creating something sturdy, beautiful, and useful—and naming it for her brother—she is honoring him with her actions as well as her words.

AS
A
FATHER

AS A FATHER

One early October afternoon, eight-year-old Abby stepped off the bus and arrived home from school, as usual. Today, however, something was off; she lacked her typical vitality and complained of being tired and not feeling well. She had a mild cough and said that her body ached all over. Nevertheless, she worked on her homework, ate supper, and went to bed early, hoping to feel better in the morning.

In the middle of the night, her parents were awakened by unusual sounds from their daughter's bedroom. They found Abby thrashing in her bed with her eyes looking upward and saliva flowing from the corners of her mouth. Neither of her terrified parents had ever witnessed a seizure before, and both were nearly paralyzed with fright.

They immediately called emergency medical service, which soon arrived, even though it felt like an eternity.

The EMTs started an IV to help control Abby's seizures, and although the medication slowed down her body movements, electronic monitoring of her brain waves at the hospital soon suggested that she remained in constant seizures.

Over the next two days, hospital medical personnel performed numerous imaging procedures and an extensive medical workup, but nothing explained the cause of her seizures. Abby did not regain consciousness during this initial hospitalization, nor did her seizures stop. Due to the seriousness of her condition, she was transported by air-flight to the regional children's hospital.

When Abby arrived at the children's hospital, a team of specialists from neurology, infectious disease, and critical care immediately began searching for the source of Abby's underlying disease. Was it the onset of a neurodegenerative disorder? Meningitis? An infection? Test after test, procedure after procedure, image after image—nothing provided a key to unlock the secret that eluded her care providers.

As Abby continued to have seizures, doctors suggested that a medically induced coma might give her brain a chance to rest and possibly heal. Her brain would be electronically monitored to see if the pattern of seizures would slow down or stop. The parents agreed to this plan, as it seemed the last resort.

Abby's father remained by her bedside. He would leave for short periods to sleep and eat, but rarely was he missing from the Pediatric Intensive Care Unit (PICU). He held her hand and talked to her, even though she was not consciously aware of his presence.

Her father described Abby as a quiet child with a winsome smile and kind heart. He posted pictures of her around the bedside so that caregivers could see her in a healthy state; the photographs ranged from tap dance recitals to clowning with her friends.

Abby's father had always felt that she was wise beyond her years—an old soul in a child's body. Simultaneously, he also thought of her as his "baby" since she was conceived several years after the arrival of her two older, rowdy brothers. Pride glistened in his eyes when he talked about their relationship.

At times, the father dwelled on his guilt over imperfect parenting; at other times, he reminisced about building doll houses, playing softball, sharing ice cream, talking with imaginary friends, helping with homework, and laughing at cartoons.

Although Abby's father, Steve, was deeply religious, his beliefs didn't lessen his suffering. He was visibly distressed and often cried. He openly expressed his grief with loud prayers and the constant question, "Why is this happening to my child?" The depth of his sadness was felt throughout the unit by staff and other parents.

Doctors repeatedly tried to reverse Abby's coma by cutting back on the medication, but each attempt resulted in renewed seizure activity. Specialists from hospitals throughout the country were consulted, but they could offer no other treatment options and hope for recovery grew dim. Doctors finally informed her parents of her deteriorating condition and probable death.

Shortly thereafter, the head physician in the PICU contacted the unit psychologist who was providing support for the family. Several of the nurses and other staff members expressed serious concerns about Abby's father.

After hearing his daughter's worsening prognosis, Steve's mood had become inexplicably positive; he proclaimed loudly that his daughter would be healed, wake up, and hug him. He even gave a specific date for her recovery.

The staff believed he was in denial about his daughter's possible death, and they were afraid that he was "mentally losing it" and would "fall apart" when she died.

The psychologist, who talked with the family daily, asked Steve about his understanding of Abby's condition. He repeated the physicians' statements concerning the gravity of his daughter's condition and the probability of her death. It was clear that he understood the severity of the situation.

Nevertheless, Steve continued to verbally express his hope. And he thought that, the more he expressed hope, the more the medical staff members were consistently responsive to Abby. The staff no longer avoided stopping by her bedside, and they met regularly with the family, even though nothing medically changed.

At the same time, many of the staff still believed that Steve would fall apart at Abby's death. Some worried that their presence was giving him false hope about her condition.

As expected, Abby was eventually removed from life sustaining equipment, and the family spent a night holding and rocking her. Early in the morning, as the sun's rays shone through the skylights of the unit, Abby died.

Had Steve been deluding himself? No. As he explained it much later, he said, "One of the most painful parts about Abby's dying was knowing that I could do nothing physically to prevent her death." This knowledge had left him feeling totally helpless and out of control.

"Suddenly," he related, "in the middle of my distress, a healing thought came to me. I would keep the medical staff engaged in Abby's care if I showed that I had not lost hope." He believed his expression of hope would encourage medical staff not to give up on his daughter. "I knew it was all that I could do, and if she did not make it, I would have done everything I could," he remarked.

After Abby died, Steve emerged from behind the curtain in front of his daughter's bed. He was calm and completely at peace. He knew that there would be difficult times ahead and felt incredible sadness over his loss. But his belief that his expressions of hope had kept care providers engaged brought him a comfort that altered his grief forever.

AS
A
CHAPLAIN

AS A CHAPLAIN

When Sarah was a freshman in college, her scores on a personality test revealed a telling pattern of traits. She scored high as a lover of the arts, a deep thinker, and a dreamer. The test also indicated a strong commitment to social justice and an intense desire to help others. Additionally, it showed an unlimited energy to study and read—which in Sarah's case, meant finding the trail toward God.

As a child, Sarah was frail. She was born prematurely, weighing less than 6 pounds, and, for the first two years of her life, she had digestive problems that included frequent projectile vomiting. Her weak immune system made her susceptible to all types of infections and childhood diseases. Her fragile constitution naturally worried her parents, who worked hard to keep her healthy. "My dad carried me outside on a pillow," she recalled, "singing to me and exposing me to fresh air."

When she was four, Sarah was the victim of a vicious dog attack. Her face was badly torn, and she still vividly remembers the dog's big teeth and being stitched up in the emergency room. After that trauma, she had recurrent nightmares of threatening monsters throughout childhood. Little could she have guessed then how important dreams would become to her life and her life's work.

Sarah's medical history had two significant influences on her early development. First, she formed a deep appreciation of nature. She loved playing outside in the woods, smelling honeysuckle, splashing in the creek, and going barefooted. To this day, she remembers how terrible it felt to be sick and forced to stay inside when she wanted to be outside playing. "I never forgot those vivid memories of freedom when I was in nature," she said.

Secondly, Sarah became a voracious reader. When she was sick at home, she read constantly. She found solace in the quietness of her room with a good book. She quickly outgrew the town library, as she would be reading eight to ten books at any one time. In the first grade, she had a special stool she climbed to reach the sixth-grade books that matched her advanced reading skills. Her parents enrolled their intellectually precocious child in a program for academically gifted children where she thrived.

As she grew, she became healthier, as well. Loving family and community surrounded her, and there were few things, other than strange dogs, to fear. She felt unconditional love from her paternal grandmother and cherished her embraces. Her grandmother, who had known great suffering and had deep faith, made the world safe. "People felt comfortable with her," Sarah said. "They would tell her their life stories because she created a sense of security."

Sarah described her extended family as "spiritual people" with different hues of faith. "The environment created by my family allowed me to develop a strong sense of trust," she recalled. "Not until I later studied the theologian James Fowler, who contended that trust is essential in forming a belief in an unseen God as well as being essential for love, did I realize how important those early relationships were for me in my spiritual development."

When Sarah went to college, she was aware of her spirituality but not necessarily in religious terms. She remained very attached to the natural world. "I always knew that I was a part of all that is," she commented.

Pulled by both her intellectual curiosity and her need to help people, Sarah earned a Master's in Divinity as well as training in pastoral care. Ever the intellectual reader, she focused on Hebrew and Greek languages.

A lifelong lover of puzzles, she was intrigued by archeology, especially studies involving symbols in ancient Hebrew life.

Sarah followed an academic path and taught university religion courses for 10 years, including a course in medical ethics. She found herself frequently talking about spirituality in the context of her ethics course and eventually decided to return to her earlier spiritual love, pastoral care. She signed up for further training in a hospital-based pastoral care program. "Any time I was on-call during training," Sarah reflected, "the beeper always went off for pediatric intensive care and oncology units. After a few months, I decided this was, indeed, a message for me."

During her pastoral care residency, Sarah found that pediatric units were, indeed, a perfect fit. She helped families of dying babies develop rituals based on each family's spiritual tradition. She talked with the family about how much love they had unleashed on the world that wouldn't have happened without their baby. She encouraged families to develop stories about simple things such as "how they came to name the baby" or "whose feet the child inherited" to mark the importance of the infant on the family.

Sarah often found that older children could not verbalize their feelings. Their fears frequently erupted in dreams especially appearing as giants and monsters.

This was something she could understand both clinically and, because of her childhood trauma, on a personal level. As her work progressed, she came to appreciate even more the importance of dreams in children's spiritual life.

After completing her pastoral care residency, Sarah accepted a position with a local Hospice, providing grief counseling for adults. Shortly thereafter, a pediatric program was developed, and Sarah eventually spent all her time with pediatric patients.

One day, Sarah received a request to work with Katie, a seven-year-old child with an inoperable brain tumor. By the time they met, Katie had lost the ability to move or speak. She could barely open her mouth to swallow; she could not smile or make other facial movements. She could move her eyes, though, and she made distinctive sounds that reflected laughter or sorrow.

Katie had been having nightmares, and Sarah began to do dreamwork with her. First, though, she had to learn how to interact with her, and Katie taught her how. The child would move her eyes up and down for "yes" and side to side for "no." She would roll her eyes for "another thought."

Sarah would give Katie four or five story beginnings for a dream such as "I was playing, or sleeping, or drawing, or eating, or reading." That was followed by choices for location, people present, and the characters' actions. If Sarah got stuck trying to figure out Katie's story, she would say letters of the alphabet, and Katie would phonetically spell a key word with her eyes.

Sarah remembered a typical dream of Katie's. "The little girl was playing outside in the backyard. She heard a sound inside the house and ran in the backdoor to the kitchen. There was a big, green monster. The mother and the little girl tried to reach each other, but they were blocked by the monster."

There was little question who—or what—that monster was.

At times, Sarah, the puzzle solver, had to make educated guesses, but interpretation became easier and quicker. Over the next 18 months, the dream work continued. Sarah pinned a dream-catcher on the side of Katie's pillow, and Katie would roll her eyes toward the dream-catcher if she had a frightening dream she wanted to tell.

Since Katie couldn't draw, Sarah started sketching Katie's stories. Sarah's drawing skills were limited to little stick figures, but they were recognizable to Katie. Often the drawings prompted a distinct sound of gurgling laughter from Katie.

The artwork expanded to include family portraits made from handprints and footprints of each family member, dipped into paint and pressed onto canvas. Katie loved the family portraits as she saw the uniqueness of her hands and feet.

The intimate relationship between Sarah and Katie grew stronger with every meeting. Remembering Katie, Sarah described her as the "most courageous child I have ever known. Her ability to cope was incredible."

Eventually, Katie began experiencing more difficulty breathing as the tumor pressed against her brainstem. One day, she struggled for breath as her lungs filled with fluids and clearly wanted to share the terror she was experiencing. Katie initially spelled out the word "angels" with her eyes. Sarah gave Katie several color choices to describe them, including white, pink, and purple, but she could not figure out the color until Katie spelled out "silver." And not only were they silver, they were "shiny silver." And then Katie rolled her eyes until Sarah somehow realized that she was trying to describe the action of a "hug." After several guesses, it became clear that Katie wanted Sarah to "ask the shiny silver angels if they would hug her the next time."

"Rarely have I stood in that priestly role and felt so helpless," Sarah recalled with deep emotion. "Yet, here was the calling to stand in that role and make a request for Katie."

Several weeks later, Sarah went camping in the mountains and had a dream about Katie. When she awoke, she knew Katie was gone. She was not surprised when she received the news of Katie's death.

Sarah was unable to attend the funeral but later went to visit Katie's mother. The first object she saw during her visit was the family portrait of handprints that Katie's mother had framed. As she sat with Katie's mother, she was able to intently listen to and understand her sadness, but Sarah knew by the tightening in her own chest that she herself was in trouble. On her way home, she had to pull off the highway as she wept uncontrollably.

From then on, Sarah repeatedly found herself thinking about Katie's suffering. She grieved that Katie never had a chance just to be a child, to be able to go outside and play. Sarah could not get past Katie's death. The thoughts persisted night and day.

She tried to "ground" herself in activities that were healing. Sarah meditated, prayed, engaged in visual imagery of the natural world, talked with others, practiced tai chi, spent time outdoors, and sought the help of other spiritual counselors.

Nothing worked.

And then, one night, she had a dream. She saw Katie in a casket. Her eyes opened and she sat up. She had mobility that Sarah had never seen. Katie twirled in place and did a ballerina dance. For the first time, Sarah heard Katie's voice. It said, "Look at me."

Sarah woke up smiling. Somehow, it was clear that Katie was no longer suffering. Sarah realized that "Katie's body died and the suffering was not real anymore except in *my mind*." At that moment, something within her changed, and she no longer felt her deep distress. She could appreciate Katie's bravery and engagement with life, despite all its limitations.

She never experienced the same despair again and was able to hold the memory of Katie and her stories as a beautiful, sacred trust.

AS
A
DAUGHTER

AS A DAUGHTER

Lorraine was a child-bride at 16 when she eloped with a 23-year-old man who thought she was 18. They were described as "beach kids from Ventura," and their marriage, with its emotional ups and downs, had felt a lot like a "yoyo" to her. The couple had settled in central California where her husband's family had sent him to manage land they owned.

Lorraine and her husband struggled to raise three children in the middle of the depression. Somehow, they survived; in 1945, the youngest of their three children was 15 and almost grown. Lorraine had gone to work outside the home and was enjoying her position as a secretary for the water district. The family was finally getting on its feet financially.

Lorraine was finished having children.

But a fourth pregnancy occurred, unplanned, the result of a World War II peace celebration (the forgotten diaphragm was found under a pillow the next morning). Lorraine had strongly considered an abortion and even tried several home remedies without success. She felt guilty that she didn't want the baby and remained extremely conflicted about having another child, even until the onset of her labor pains.

The baby, Cheryl, had a long and difficult birth. During the delivery, the doctor discovered that Lorraine had placenta previa, causing the discharge of the placenta before, rather than after, Cheryl's birth. Lorraine hemorrhaged severely, and the doctor's hope that the baby's downward pressure would stop the bleeding didn't occur. After six hours—a delay due to the rural location of the hospital—an emergency C-section was performed. Cheryl was expected to die or, if she survived, to be severely brain damaged.

Surprising everyone, Cheryl not only survived, she thrived.

From the moment Cheryl was born, Lorraine was compulsively vigilant against any unexpected things happening to her daughter. She feared the wrath of God; afraid that as punishment for her ambivalence about the pregnancy, God would allow her to love Cheryl and then take her away.

When Cheryl was a year old, her parents moved from the small community where she was born to the family farm. Her father split time between farming and working for the local water district. All the older children had left home, and Lorraine felt that she could protect Cheryl in this environment, where she would be isolated, safe, and raised as an "only child."

Lorraine was at a loss as to how to nurture Cheryl. The large size of Lorraine's family of origin didn't allow her *own* mother to give significant time and attention to each child; there were 10 children with seven surviving to adulthood. At the time of Lorraine's birth, two of the siblings had recently died, including her mother's favorite daughter. Her grieving mother did not bond with Lorraine, leaving the child to experience little care and tenderness as a child.

And Lorraine wasn't the last child in the family. As she matured, she was put in charge of her youngest sibling, Grace, who was considered to be the "baby" of the family. Lorraine was charged with protecting Grace from any harm—not an easy task, since Grace was a free spirit who did what she wanted. In fact, the family eventually named her "Dis-Grace."

As a mother, Lorraine was determined that Cheryl wouldn't meet this fate, and she pushed Cheryl for perfection, especially in education. She taught her daughter to read, write, and calculate numbers before she entered school. Throughout Cheryl's school years, there were nightly sessions of collaborative homework to make sure that all her academic work was done correctly. Cheryl felt her mother was incredibly smart. Remarkably, Lorraine was totally self-educated, although most people thought she had a college degree. She was an avid reader who had read 90% of the books in the local library. Having her daughter achieve at a high level was very important to her.

Lorraine was an activist who rallied for speed limits on the roads, fought over the spending of school funds, and promoted cultural activities including securing Beverly Sills to perform in their small community. Yet, she never seemed to understand her own power and her impact on people. She had difficulty emotionally relating to others, although she remained with her spouse for 74 years and had a close bond with her sisters.

Socially, Lorraine was insecure and self-conscious about herself and Cheryl. She always wanted everything about her daughter to "look right." When Cheryl's hair had some premature gray streaks, Lorraine dyed them to cover the gray. Once, an ash brown rinse turned Cheryl's hair green, and Lorraine was so horrified that she refused to let Cheryl leave the house.

Lorraine was rigid—to the point of being punitive—in her unrealistic expectations of her daughter. When

Cheryl was five, for example, the family scheduled a first-time trip to see her older brother's new home. Cheryl was so delighted and excited she couldn't eat. Without a second thought, Lorraine refused to let Cheryl go as punishment for not eating. Cheryl remembers becoming hysterical and, at that young age, being totally confused by her mother's actions.

Throughout Cheryl's childhood, Lorraine continued to be haunted by guilt and the old fear of something happening to her daughter. During a family fishing outing, Lorraine, out of her fear, tied Cheryl to a bridge railing so she wouldn't fall off. Lorraine's double-edged emotional attitude toward her daughter was fueled by both protective fear and near-abusive expectations of perfection. In truth, they were the two sides of the same coin: she had to produce a perfect (and safe) child to somehow atone for the ambivalence she had felt about even having the child.

Unsurprisingly, Cheryl describes growing up with her mother as "tortuous." Cheryl remembers her mother belittling her and crowns Lorraine as "being the queen of left-handed compliments." The initial statement was always "warm and fuzzy," followed by the inevitable "jab." Her mother would begin, "I really like that skirt," and then follow with "it covers up your ugly knees." She would say to her daughter, "I like you in that color," and then add "it makes you look less sallow." Cheryl didn't realize how demeaning these passive-aggressive statements were until she left home.

Because she spent most of her time with her parents and without babysitters or friends, Cheryl didn't see how other mothers behaved with their daughters. Cheryl had difficulty remembering positive interactions with her mother. She recalled, "Mother and I did not do 'girly' things together. There were few fun moments like other girls described, and there was little physical touch. Mother was emotionally tone deaf." Cheryl denies any physical harm by her mother but rather remembers, "It was just this whacky, verbal, undercutting (but pushing for perfection) stuff."

Cheryl felt totally out of control in her relationship with her mother and became an angry child. She remembers slamming the door to her room so hard that the doorjamb came off. At times, she refused to talk with Lorraine and would hold up in her room for days.

Reflecting on her childhood, Cheryl believes that she was saved by her father's acceptance and unconditional love. He believed in her. He taught her how to paint, drive a car, put up a fence, and roof a house; he had confidence in her ability and appreciated her inquisitiveness. She loved talking with him; they walked in the orchard at night with eyes on the stars, discussing the likelihood of life on other planets. They sat on the roof and watched for Sputnik, talking about what would come next in space exploration. She treasured their time together.

Her older brother also provided needed emotional support, especially his willingness to stand up for her when he came around the family. He was her champion. Both her father and her brother "gave me the idea that there was life after childhood."

Cheryl eventually reached adulthood. After graduating from high school, she left for college where she majored in political science. She met her future spouse and, over Lorraine's objections, married during her junior year. Lorraine adored her son-in-law but had not wanted Cheryl to marry. She withdrew financial support, although she and Cheryl's father gave the couple a lump sum that paid for the final two years of college.

Cheryl and her spouse, Paul, joined the Peace Corps after graduation and spent their committed time in Sierra Leone. She saw people grow up in hard, difficult situations and turn out to be fine people. For the first time, she began to think that her own hard life had given her strength.

After returning to the states, the young couple had two daughters, made a lot of memories, but eventually divorced. As a single mother, Cheryl consciously decided that she would parent differently from her mother. She wanted the girls to feel loved and to be "whoever they were."

But Cheryl found that nurturing didn't come naturally—unsurprising, since she had an insufficient maternal role model. She tried to be more loving and caring like her father, and she remains grateful to her daughters who developed the "two-ask-rule." The girls would ask to do something, and Cheryl's immediate response was "no." She had always been told "no" by Lorraine as a child, and it was an automatic reply. The girls would then ask a second time, which gave Cheryl time to reflect on her decision and change her mind if appropriate.

Cheryl delighted in the girls and encouraged their pursuits. She laughed with them, cried with them, and listened to them. She worked hard to give them the affirmation she didn't receive from her mother and hoped they never experienced her feeling of not having the "mother she wanted."

Going home was painful, and she often developed a throbbing headache as soon as she saw the city limits' sign. She wanted to go, however. The family home was a base for Cheryl to go and see old friends. During one of the yearly visits when the girls were young, Lorraine told one of her granddaughters, "I am sorry that you do not live closer so that I can help you with your speech impediment." That passive-aggressive statement, so like the comments her mother made to her, resulted in even less contact: Cheryl was sorry only that she would miss spending time with her dad. After the girls were grown, Cheryl moved to the East Coast and had limited contact with Lorraine.

As an adult, Cheryl thought she would probably never resolve things with her mother. Therapy helped put a different perspective on the relationship, giving her the knowledge and confidence that she had more power and control with her aging parents than she had thought. She realized that they needed her more than she needed them, and she became more capable of deflecting Lorraine's negative comments. Occasionally, she would even challenge some of her mother's problematic assumptions.

Despite—or perhaps because of—their difficult relationship, Cheryl greatly feared her mother's death. She believed that death would freeze the relationship, and any improvement would then be impossible. She was terrified of the finality of her mother's death and how she might be overwhelmed emotionally.

At the age of 90, Lorraine had a stroke, paralyzing the right side of her body. She could not write and could only mutter a few words. Speech was very difficult. She eventually became bedridden and required care in a nursing facility.

Cheryl found herself calling Lorraine daily, and she was grateful that the nursing assistant held the phone next to Lorraine's ear. Lorraine listened but never said anything inappropriate, which was delightful to Cheryl. Her mother facially appeared to enjoy hearing about what Cheryl was doing. Cheryl then began writing letters regularly to her mother and was able to express some of the things that she had long wanted to say. To her relief, there was neither negative feedback nor inappropriate comments. Cheryl gradually lost her fear of retribution, and Lorraine was becoming the accepting, positive mother that Cheryl had always wanted.

The week before Lorraine died, Cheryl and her older sister were able to sit by their mother's bedside and respond to her needs. They played opera music and told old jokes and family stories. Without realizing it, Cheryl experienced her mother in a different way because of these late interactions.

When Lorraine died, Cheryl was surprised that she was able to grieve, honestly, for her mother. She felt genuine emotion and sadness, and she was able to remember and cherish the good things that her mother had done. In that moment, the thought came to her that she could mourn her mother, *as she was*, a complex person with strengths and weaknesses.

She may never have had the loving, nurturing mother she felt she needed, but she *had* had a mother and had finally been able to connect with her, with all her flaws, in a genuine way.

Somehow, this was enough.

AS
A
THERAPIST

AS A THERAPIST

For most of her career, Ellen worked as a psychologist in a pediatric intensive care unit (PICU) serving children who had experienced trauma, surgery, or complications from acute or chronic illness. She received requests from the medical staff that generally involved helping families cope with trauma, providing direct support for the child, and doing grief work. She described the intensive care unit as a highly stressful environment, typified by constant sounds of alarms, unfamiliar equipment, intensive monitoring, and critical decision-making by the staff and family. Anxiety created by the threat of a child's possible death was palpable.

Children usually didn't stay in the PICU for long: they were transferred to less critical care units or, in some cases, did not survive. As Ellen participated in medical rounds on a daily basis, the few children who stayed for a prolonged period of time would send up a red flag for her, because a child's long stay in the unit took its toll on families. One day, her eyes were drawn to an adolescent patient somewhat isolated in a corner bed of the unit. She had noticed him before, as his parents were constantly by his bedside. He appeared more responsive than most patients, and her curiosity was piqued about his circumstances. Ellen hadn't received a request to provide services for him, so she inquired about his condition.

She was told that the sixteen-year-old had been diagnosed with Goodpasture's Syndrome, a rare disorder in which the body's immune system mistakenly destroys healthy tissue in the kidneys and lungs. By the time he was diagnosed and treated, he had suffered severe kidney damage requiring a kidney transplant. Without a second thought, his mother donated her kidney, and the surgery was successful. Following surgery, however, it was impossible to remove his breathing tube due to his high level of anxiety. When attempts were made, he became anxious and required excessive sedation, thus preventing removal of the tube. Ellen was asked to work with the adolescent.

The parents appeared exhausted and worried about their son, Kevin. They had a quiet manner and were open to any suggestions that might help him. Ellen suggested relaxation techniques to decrease both his anxiety and the use of sedation during the removal of his breathing tube. She explained a visualization technique that would use memory of an event or place that might be relaxing or peaceful for him. Because of the breathing tube, he was unable to talk about or offer any possibilities. His parents talked about a memorable trip to Walt Disney World and gave Ellen details that might be easy for him to imagine. However, after she asked Kevin to visualize the event, he became more agitated.

His parents then described their son's car, a restored magenta Malibu with black interior. The car was kept in immaculate condition and housed on a covered concrete pad specifically built for its protection. When he was not in the hospital, the car was the center of Kevin's life. Ellen asked him to imagine sitting in the car, focusing on its sights, smells, and sounds. Through his imagination, he took a drive through the rural countryside where he lived. He became deeply relaxed.

Ellen asked the medical staff to call her when they were ready to try removing Kevin's tube again. The next morning, a 6:00 a.m. call woke her from a deep sleep. She dressed and immediately drove to the hospital. Kevin was able to relax by visualizing a ride in his car, and the tube was successfully removed. He was freed from his tether and moved to a room on a regular hospital floor.

Ellen followed him through his hospitalization, which was not an easy course. There were constant medication changes and fear about possible rejection of the kidney. After being in a prone position for so long, he was so weak that even walking took effort. He was eventually discharged home with medications he would have to take the rest of his life. He and his family had hope, however, that he could return to normal adolescent activities such as waxing and buffing the Malibu, hanging out with friends, and finishing high school. More importantly, they hoped he would have a long life.

A couple of years later, Ellen received a called from Kevin's nephrologist. Kevin's transplanted kidney had failed, he was on dialysis, and needed another transplant. The doctor was concerned about his depressed mood. Ellen agreed to work with Kevin on an outpatient basis with the caveat that they would discuss the possibility of declining another transplant. His physician expressed some reservation, as she felt a transplant was his only option, but agreed to be open to whatever Kevin, who was now of legal age, decided.

Ellen saw Kevin for therapy in conjunction with his nephrology visits. His mood was initially understandably depressed, since the loss of his kidney represented a loss of normal activities for him. His strongest desire was not to stand out or be different. Like adolescent patients with cancer who often express more distress over hair loss than possible mortality, Kevin just wanted to drive his car, go to school, and be with his friends.

Kevin tended to be quiet and reserved in sessions, but often the silent moments seemed to be a source of respite for him. He reflected on his pain and suffering during the previous surgery and the option of not having a second transplant. He talked about dying and what the dying process might be like, as well as his beliefs about an afterlife. He was acutely aware that his acquiring a kidney would mean that someone else and their family would have suffered a tragic loss. Making a decision about the transplant was complex and difficult, especially when he considered his parents. Kevin was extremely close to them and felt that not having another transplant would be letting them down. As long as there was a chance for survival, he decided, he wanted to move forward.

As the months passed, Kevin's condition deteriorated, and he needed a cane to walk. His breathing was labored. He could no longer drive, and he seemed more resigned about his condition. He was now on the transplant list for both a kidney and lung transplant due to further complications of his disease.

After being on the transplant list for about a year, Kevin received a kidney and lung transplant. Initially, surgery appeared successful, even though Kevin was in critical condition and highly vulnerable to any infection. His mood remained hopeful and, despite his obvious suffering, he made few complaints.

Although he appeared to be recovering, an insidious underlying rejection process of both the lung and kidney set in. One morning, Ellen received a page from the PICU staff that Kevin's condition had worsened. The day's plan was to try all possible procedures that might save his life.

Ellen met his exhausted, distraught parents outside his hospital room. They had been with him all night. They said the doctors' news was discouraging and they feared for their son's survival. They asked if Ellen would stay with him throughout the day, as they could not watch any further procedures with him.

She agreed.

The multiple teams of specialists, nurses, and other staff began their many complex procedures on Kevin. Incisions were made, tubes were inserted, machines took over essential body functions, and the constant alarms noisily filled the air. Tubes were in every orifice of his body and there was blood everywhere. Kevin was given constant transfusions, but his bodily fluids seemed to be irreplaceable. Medical staff moved him from room to room as procedures were often followed by the need for imagery to determine the effectiveness of each intervention.

Specialists shouted instructions in loud, stern voices. The mood was agitated, yet somehow seemed as sterile as the bright lights and equipment in the rooms. There was a level of tension that Ellen had not experienced with Kevin's care in the past. Although Kevin was unconscious, she held his hand, stood close by, and provided reassurance by talking about his Malibu and family. Both touch and a familiar voice seemed to calm him. Ellen strongly believed that Kevin could still experience comfort, even though unconscious, and several times that day, the medical staff affirmed the need for spiritual comfort for him.

Kevin was ashen and made no sound or movement. As the day wore on, the doctors became discernably more discouraged, and they began commenting that they had done everything they could do. After 10 to 12 hours of valiant efforts to save his life, Kevin was pronounced dead.

It was a heartbreaking end to a young life.

Ellen was unable to attend his funeral but later drove to the rural area where Kevin had lived. It was a sunny morning, and the light shone through trees that lined the country road. She wanted to see his parents and brother again and to provide possible comfort. They seemed to be at the point in grief when the finality of death had become painfully real. Even in their grief, they greeted Ellen warmly and wanted to share photo albums of Kevin when he was a child. It was important to them that Ellen learn about who he was outside the hospital. Pictures of him camping, riding in a Soap Box Derby car, and playing with his brother on the beach gave Ellen a glimpse of his early years when he was healthy and happy. Before she left, Ellen asked if she could see the Malibu. It was sitting in its special, protected place with no evidence of having been moved or driven.

Returning to work, Ellen found herself experiencing flashbacks of Kevin's last day of life. The sights and sounds of those invasive procedures invaded her waking and sleeping. She felt she was once again in the room as the staff frantically attempted to save his life. It was difficult to focus on work; it seemed impossible to rest.

Ellen sometimes felt strangely numb and found it hard to express her grief openly. It seemed impossible to cry. Ellen didn't know if her reaction was an accumulation of so much death and trauma experienced in the unit or a specific reaction to Kevin's death, but she did know his death had been different and especially difficult for her. She found herself constantly fatigued and sleeping through most weekends. Ellen self-diagnosed post-traumatic stress symptoms and hoped that the symptoms would eventually go away.

Shortly thereafter, Ellen had the opportunity to do clinical research, and she decided it might be emotionally helpful to take a break from clinical work. As the months and years passed, the frequency of her memories of Kevin decreased, but the thoughts she did have of him were always negative and distressing. She eventually returned to trauma work, but her own trauma with his death had not resolved.

One morning, Ellen was walking down the hospital corridor to see a new patient. Without warning and without any effort on her part, Ellen experienced an unexplained healing. She suddenly saw Kevin again, but this time he was driving the Malibu down the country road with windows open, hair blowing, and a smile on his face. He appeared healthy and happy. It brought a sense of peace that she hadn't felt in years. From that moment on, her thoughts about him changed from centering on his suffering to focusing on his joy in life. The distressful thoughts stopped. What remained was comfort.

Now, when she sees him, he is driving down the highway, hair blowing, free of tethers and pain.

REFERENCES

1. Kubler-Ross, E. (1969). *On death and dying*. New York: Scribner.

2. Lewis, C. S. (1961). *A grief observed*. United Kingdom: Faber and Faber.

3. Neimeyer, R. A. (1998). *Lessons of loss: A guide to coping*. New York: McGraw-Hill.

4. Bearison, D. J. (2006). *When treatment fails: How medicine cares for dying children*. New York: Oxford University Press.

5. Krementz, J. (1999). *How it feels when a parent dies*. New York: Alfred A. Knopf.